AF454116

WRITTEN BY
RAGHAV AGGARWAL

Don't Be Upset, Lovely Owlet!

ILLUSTRATED BY
YOGESH MAHAJAN

Baby barn owl had trouble on his mind.
"Why am I so ugly?"
The answer he badly wanted to find!

Mom, look at piglet, lamb, pup, and bunny.
Why am I not cute like them? I look funny!

Look at my flat face and feathers so dense.
The way I am — does that make sense?"

Mother Owl said, "Let's talk about
not so cute animals and birds
who grow up attractive in this magical world!

Cubs are pink, furless, and blind,
helpless and petite, difficult to find!
Just like you, they may say,
'Mom, we look so ugly!'
But see the giant panda, who looks so lovely!

Larvae are black with coloured spots and bands,
like tiny crocs feeding on insects wherever they can!
Just like you, they may say,
'Mom, we look so ugly!'
But see the red lady bug, who looks so lovely!

Caterpillars look like a barbed-wire fence.
Head or tail is anyone's guess, with red stripes so immense!
Just like you, they may say, 'Mom, we look so ugly!'
But see the clear Glasswing butterfly, who looks so lovely!

Caterpillars with white and fleshy skin
give a cold impression but are fiery within!
Just like you, they may say,
'Mom, we look so ugly!'
But see the atlas moth with wingspan so lovely!

Parrot chicks seem alien-like or like roast chickens,
without colours, as if disease-stricken!
Just like you, they may say,
'Mom, we look so ugly!'
But see the colourful kea parrots with shades so lovely!

You'll grow up to be big and strong.
Those feathers will help you fly quietly!" said Mom.
"With a face that looks like a heart,
those deep, dark eyes aim like a dart!

The little owlet was not worried anymore,
ready to be awake all night and
through the whole day snore!

Shining like a twinkling star in the night,
he glided through the sky like a ball of white!

Thanks, Mom. I'm not ugly. Now I know!
It is time to hoot, twit-hoo, twit-hoo. Here I go!

Colour your imagination!

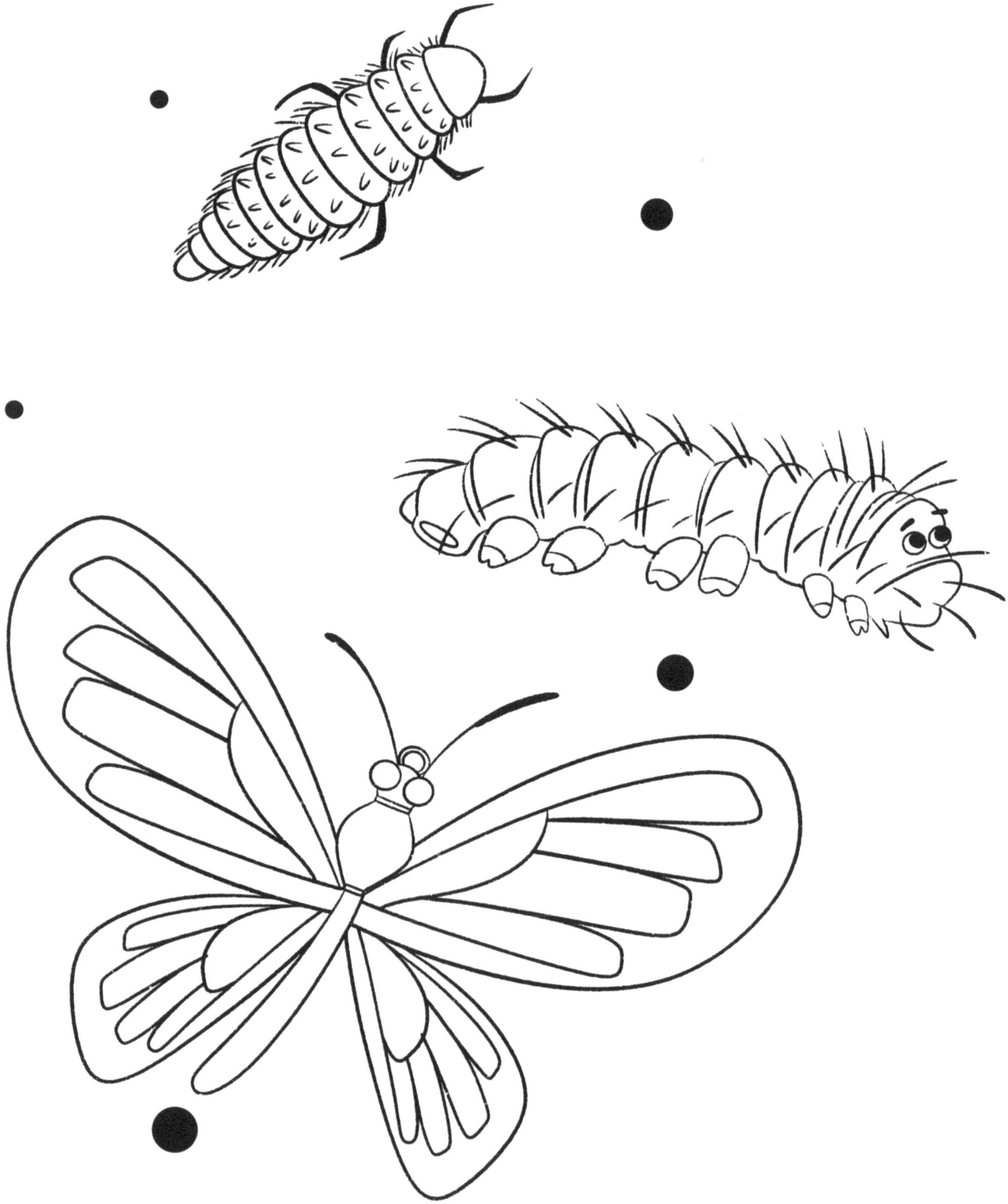

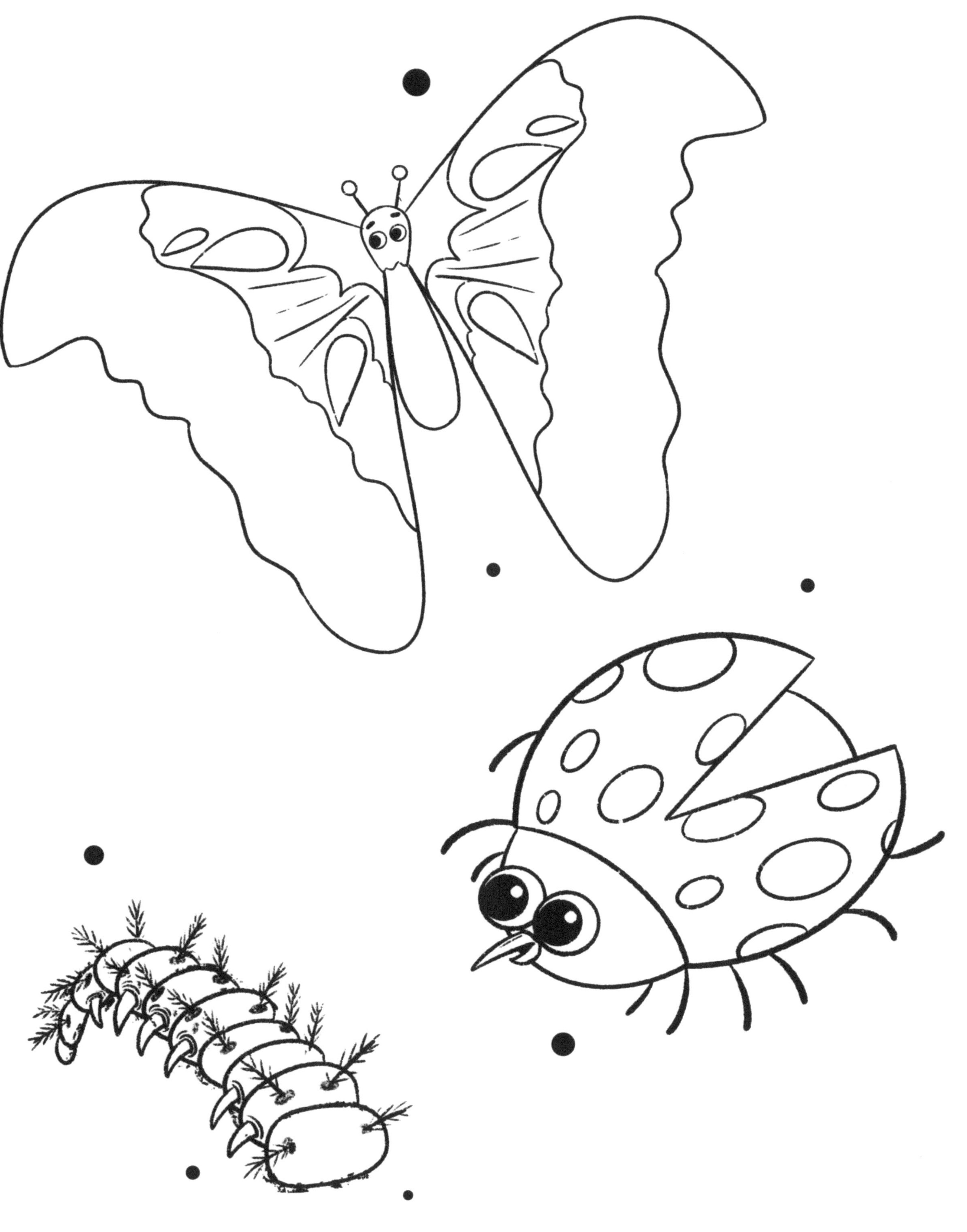